The Boy Who Could Fly

David A. Hill

HELBLING LANGUAGES
www.helblinglanguages.com

The Boy Who Could Fly
by David A. Hill

First published 2010

ISBN 978-3-85272-158-3

The publishers would like to thank the following for their kind permission to reproduce the following photographs and other copyright material: The publishers would like to thank the following for their kind permission to reproduce the following photographs and other copyright material: **Shutterstock** p7, p8, p90 (flying bird); **Wikimedia Commons** p90 (Leonardo da Vinci's drawing).

Series editor Maria Cleary
Illustrated by Valentina Russello
Activities by David A. Hill
Design and layout by BNC comunicazione
Printed by Athesia

About this Book

For the Student

🎧 Listen to the story and do some activities on your Audio CD
🎧 End of the listening excerpt
🗩 Talk about the story
ban• When you see the blue dot you can check the word in the glossary

For the Teacher

Go to our Readers Resource site for information on using readers and downloadable Resource Sheets, photocopiable Worksheets, Answer Keys and Tapescripts. Plus free sample tracks from the story.
www.helblingreaders.com

For lots of great ideas on using Graded Readers consult Reading Matters, the Teacher's Guide to using Helbling Readers.

Level 4 Structures

Sequencing of future tenses	*Could / was able to / managed to*
Present perfect plus *yet, already, just*	*Had to / didn't have to*
First conditional	*Shall / could* for offers
Present and past passive	*May / can / could* for permission
	Might for future possibility
How long?	*Make* and *let*
Very / really / quite	Causative *have*
	Want / ask / tell someone to do something

Structures from other levels are also included.

Contents

Meet the Author

Hello, David. Can you tell us a little about yourself?

Yes, certainly. I was born in Walsall, UK, and after school trained• and worked as a teacher in England. In 1977 I left the UK, and since then I have lived in Italy, Serbia and Hungary. I have also worked with students and teachers in 30 other countries around the world. These days I spend my time writing educational books, including original and adapted readers like this one, and training teachers of English. When I'm not working, I play in a blues band and study the natural world and art and architecture. I also read a lot and write short stories and poetry.

Where did you get the idea for this story?

I have always loved birds and the beauty of their flight. One of my oldest hobbies is birdwatching, and I have always thought how wonderful• it would be to be able to fly. The story began by thinking about what flying would be like for a person with wings, and then what problems someone who could fly might have.

What is the message of this story?

The message underneath this story is that people must be allowed to be different, and that we should be happy that there are differences. Differences are what make the world an interesting place. It is also important that we include people who are different, and accept them and make them welcome, while respecting their individuality.

Before Reading

Birds and flight

1 There are around 9700 different kinds of birds in the world today. They are all very different from each other in size, shape, the food they eat, the places they live, and the things they can do. Look at the pictures of these four birds. What do you know about them? How are they different from each other? Discuss with a partner.

a) Emperor Penguin

b) House Sparrow

c) Eagle Owl

d) Ostrich

2 **Answer these questions:**
   a) Which bird lives near people?
   b) Which bird runs very fast?
   c) Which bird lives in a cold climate?
   d) Which bird flies at night?
   e) Which bird eats fish?
   f) Which bird eats meat?
   g) Which bird can swim underwater?
   h) Which birds cannot fly?

Before Reading

1 **Most birds can fly. In order to do this, birds have different bodies from other living creatures. They have very light bones, and very big chest muscles to move their wings up and down. They also have things which other living creatures don't have: wings and feathers. Label these two pictures.**

a) .... **b)** ....

2 **People have always wanted to fly. What do you know about the history of human flight? Match the people (a-c) with the actions (1-3).**

a) ☐ Daedulus and Icarus
b) ☐ Leonardo da Vinci
c) ☐ Orville and Wilbur Wright

1 Studied flight and made drawings of different kinds of flying machines.
2 Made the first manned flight at Kittyhawk in the USA in 1903.
3 The father made wings for his son, but he flew too close to the sun, and the wax that held the feathers onto his arms melted, and the son fell into the sea.

3 **Which one of the three sets of people and events above did not really exist?**

4 Look at this picture of the man who could fly. Write a description of him. Think about how he is different from you and describe the differences.

5 How do you think it feels to be able to fly like a bird? What would be the advantages and disadvantages? Make some notes below.

Advantages	Disadvantages

6 Discuss your ideas with a partner.

Before Reading

1 **The main character in the story is Michael Broad – he is 'the boy who could fly'. He is the only person in the world who has wings and can fly. Read this extract from Chapter 2:**

> 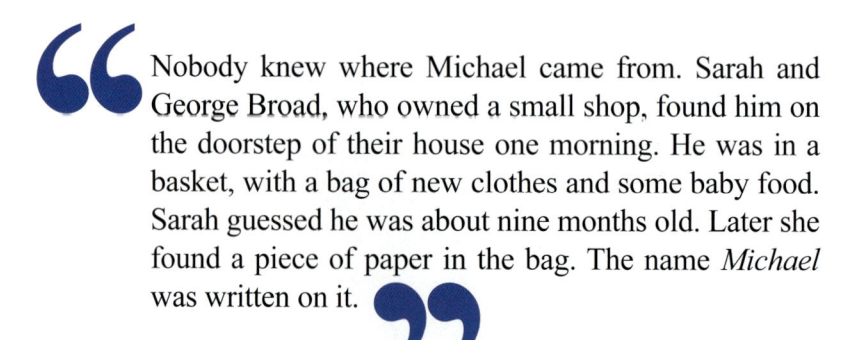 Nobody knew where Michael came from. Sarah and George Broad, who owned a small shop, found him on the doorstep of their house one morning. He was in a basket, with a bag of new clothes and some baby food. Sarah guessed he was about nine months old. Later she found a piece of paper in the bag. The name *Michael* was written on it.

Where do you think Michael came from? How could he grow wings and fly? Give reasons for your answers.

2 **In pairs look at these pictures from the story. Describe the setting of each one. What is happening in each picture? Choose one and write a detailed description. Try to imagine what happens next.**

3 Listen to this extract from the story. Draw the route the three men took on the map.

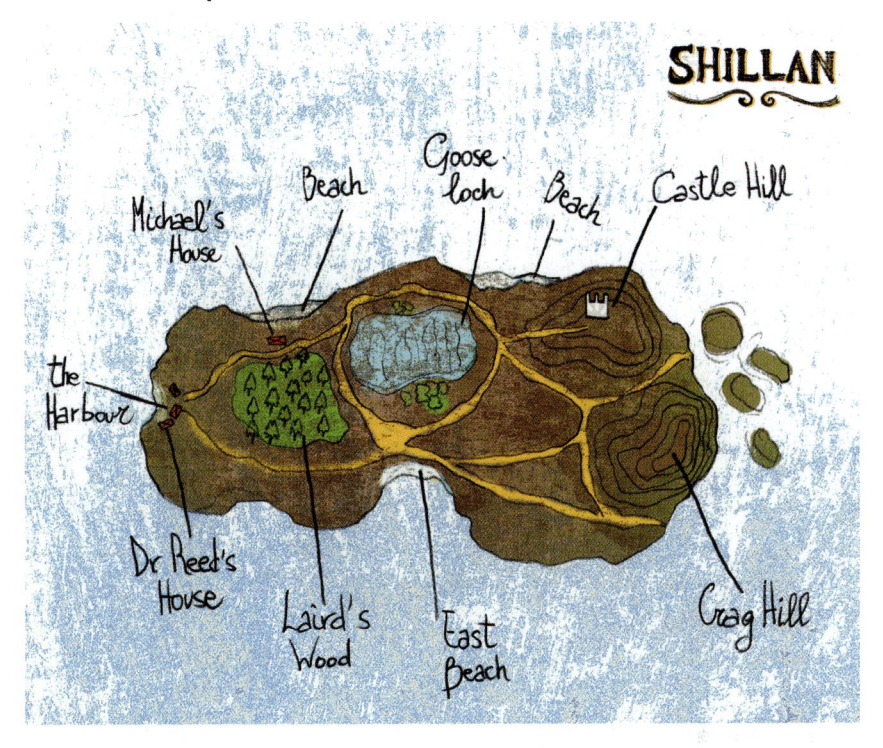

4 Now answer these questions:

a) Who are the three men?
b) Did they kill Michael?
c) What did they do with him?

5 Why do you think the men want to capture Michael? With a partner discuss possible reasons. Think of the following:

- What ability makes Michael special?
- How can the men use this ability?

Today

One hundred metres above the earth, the man who could fly moved his large white wings gently backwards and forwards.

It was very quiet up there, and the air was clean and fresh. When he looked down, he could see the village where he lived and the school where he taught. If he turned his head, he could see the park and, beyond* that, fields with cows and sheep in them.

He moved his wings a little faster and rose* higher. He could see even more now – those hills in the distance were the Bellock Hills. And that large blue shape* was Willtery Lake.

Then he began to feel a bit dizzy* and sick. He could fly quite easily at this height, but looking down at the ground so far below him always made him feel strange. Sometimes he was afraid of falling, but of course he never did. Birds don't fall to the ground, and he was like a bird.

He took one last look at the countryside, then he opened his wings wide, made a few slow circles and gracefully* flew down towards the park below.

He landed easily on his feet. After folding* his wings flat* onto his back, he put on his special extra-large jacket to cover them. Now he looked the same as everyone else. As he walked home across the grass, he thought about his supper.

Flying always gave him a good appetite*.

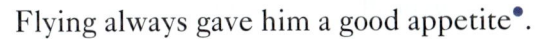

Glossary

- **appetite:** wanting to eat
- **beyond:** further away
- **dizzy:** confused; without balance
- **flat:** lying on a surface
- **folding:** making smaller (something flat)

- **gracefully:** in a smooth and beautiful way
- **rose:** moved upwards
- **shape:** form

Nobody knew where Michael came from. Sarah and George Broad, who owned• a small shop, found him on the doorstep• of their house one morning. He was in a basket with a bag of new clothes and some baby food. Sarah guessed he was about nine months old. Later she found a piece of paper in the bag. The name *Michael* was written on it.

The Broads immediately told the police about the baby. Michael's picture and details were soon in all the papers and he was even on the national news. But nobody recognised• him or came to take him back, so the Broads looked after him and a year later they adopted• him.

Adoption

The following people all have one thing in common: they were adopted. Do you know why they are famous? Discuss with a partner.

- Aristotle
- Charles Dickens
- Crazy Horse
- Edgar Allan Poe
- John Lennon
- Nelson Mandela

See if you can discover the names of other famous adopted people or adoptive parents.

Glossary

- **adopted:** took Michael into their family and legally made him their son
- **doorstep:** a small step outside the main door to a house
- **owned:** possessed; had
- **recognised:** knew who he was

Michael was happy with Sarah and George. And they were happy with him. They didn't have any children so he became the son they never had.

Michael grew up to be a nice boy. He was very popular with the customers° in the Broads' shop, and with his friends and teachers at his nursery school°. When he was old enough to understand, Sarah and George explained to him that they weren't his real parents, but he didn't mind°.

Like all children, Michael grew taller and stronger every day. He was a normal child in every way, except for the size of his chest°. His chest was very large. And it grew larger and stronger as he got older. People began to notice it. The teachers began to talk about it. The Broads began to wonder° about it.

- **chest:** the upper front part of the body
- **customers:** clients
- **he didn't mind:** it wasn't a problem for him

- **nursery school:** school for children aged between 3 and 5
- **wonder:** think; ask themselves questions

15

Going to school

Michael's life changed when he started primary school. He started feeling pains• in his back, near his shoulders. Sometimes he couldn't sleep at night because of them. The family doctor examined him but he found nothing unusual.

When Michael started his second year at school the pains got much worse, so Sarah took him to see a specialist• at the hospital. The specialist examined him and ordered x-rays. From the x-rays he could clearly see that some extra bones were growing out of Michael's shoulders. These bones were pushing against his skin and causing the pains. The doctor told Sarah to bring him back the following day, but it was too late.

That night Sarah and George were woken up by shouts from Michael's bedroom. They quickly ran to him and were shocked by what they saw. A large bone was growing out of each of his shoulders!

George called an ambulance, and an hour later Michael was back in the hospital. They x-rayed him again and several specialists examined him. George and Sarah stayed there all night and were able to see him from time to time. Between visits, the specialists asked them a lot of questions about Michael. At seven o'clock in the morning a nurse told them to go home.

'What about Michael?' asked George.

'He has to stay here,' the nurse replied.

Glossary

- **pains:** when something hurts
- **specialist:** someone who know a lot about one thing

Later that same morning he was put into an ambulance and taken to another hospital a long way away.

That day he cried because of the pains in his shoulders. He cried because he didn't know where he was. He cried because he wanted Sarah and George.

Everyone in the hospital was very nice to him. They gave him his favourite food, read him stories and let him watch television. But he was still very sad. In the evening he talked to Sarah on the phone.

'Don't worry, Michael,' she said. 'We'll come and see you tomorrow.'

Away from home

Have you ever been away from home without your family?
When was it?
How did you feel?
Share with a friend.
How do you think Michael feels?

Michael stayed in this special hospital for a year. The bones in his shoulders grew bigger, and new muscles• developed around them. After the first six months white feathers• started to grow on the bones, and it was clear to everyone, including Michael, that they were wings. Slowly he found he could move the new bones by using the muscles in his chest.

Every morning a team of doctors examined him. Then in the afternoons other doctors tried to help him to remember his past, before Sarah found him. But he couldn't remember anything. Michael didn't like staying at the hospital. The only things he liked were the lessons he had with his teacher, Mr. Smith, and the visits from George and Sarah on Sundays.

Mr Smith was a small dark man in a grey suit. He didn't teach much Maths or English. Most of the lessons were about flying because Mr Smith was really an expert on flight•.

He explained the history of flight to Michael, from Leonardo Da Vinci's experiments with flying machines to modern jet engines•. Michael learnt about birds, bats, insects and flying animals. He learnt about how the air moves, and what winds are. He drew models and diagrams. He watched films and did experiments. Soon Michael became an expert, too.

He also had to do exercises in the gym every afternoon. A big man called Pete showed him what to do, but Mr Smith and one of the doctors always watched and took notes. The exercises he did were to make his chest and new wing muscles stronger. At first they were very difficult to do, but gradually they became easier.

Glossary

- **engines:** motors
- **feather:**
- **flight:** how you fly
- **muscles:** pieces of flesh in your body that connect two bones and which you use when you make a movement

Michael flies

And then one day, nine months after Michael arrived at the special hospital, he flew for the first time. His wings were now covered with beautiful, long, white feathers. He was in the gym doing his exercises, when suddenly he rose into the air. Michael was so surprised that he stopped moving his wings and he fell to the ground.

'Try again,' Pete said. So he tried again and… YES… he could fly!!

At first, he could only lift himself a metre or two off the ground and stay there for about a minute. Then he had to rest. But his muscles got stronger, and, after a month, he could stay in the air for several minutes. It was an amazing feeling!

After that, Pete started taking Michael outside for his lessons and soon Michael learnt how to fly properly. He felt sorry for Mr Smith. His teacher knew so much about flying but couldn't actually do it himself, and he, a seven-year-old boy, could! Michael suddenly realised that he was different and special. He was the boy who could fly. Perhaps the *only* boy in the world who could fly.

The following Sunday Michael asked the nurses to take George and Sarah to a quiet little garden next to the hospital building. They were sitting on a bench waiting for him when, suddenly, he ran into the middle of the grass.

'Hi, Sarah! Hi, George!' he shouted. 'Watch me!'

He moved his big, white-feathered wings and slowly rose up in the air. Sarah and George couldn't believe their eyes! They were laughing and crying at the same time.

Escape from the hospital

Michael was tired of being in the hospital. He wanted to go home, and Sarah and George wanted him back.

'Why?' he shouted. 'Why do I have to be here? I'm sick of living in a hospital. I can fly. So what•? Let me go home!'

But every day the doctors found another reason for him to stay there.

'They'll never let me go home,' he thought. 'I'll become like a rare animal in a zoo. I'll be "the flying boy".' And he felt very unhappy.

The Broads were unhappy too. They didn't want Michael to stay in the hospital for the rest of his life. They wanted him to be like other boys of his age. So the next time that Sarah and George went to see Michael, the three of them made a plan.

The plan

What is Michael, George and Sarah's plan?
Make groups of 3. Each person is one of the characters.
Together discuss ways to get Michael out of the hospital.
Find the pros and cons of each idea.
Try and find an idea that will work.

Glossary

- **So what?:** (exclamation) What's the problem?

The following Sunday morning, George and Sarah drove to the hospital to visit Michael as usual. Sarah got out of the car and went inside, but George didn't. He stayed in the car park. Sarah went into the garden where Michael joined her. After a few minutes she went back inside. 'I forgot my glasses,' she said to the porter. 'They're in the car.'

The porter unlocked the door and let her out. Sarah walked to the car park and got into the car. A moment later, Michael flew over the high hospital wall, landed• in the car park, folded his wings, and got into the car too. George pressed his foot on the accelerator• and they raced down the road away from the hospital.

• **accelerator:** pedal you press in a car to make it go faster

• **landed:** went onto the ground

Problems at home

The porter at the hospital rang the police. And someone at the police station rang the newspapers. When George arrived home, the car was immediately surrounded by photographers and reporters• from every newspaper and television and radio station in the country. It was impossible for the three of them to get out of the car without being attacked by the journalists• and paparazzi•. They were shouting:

 'Can you give us some idea of the boy's mental state, Mrs Broad ?'

 'Mr Broad, who do you think the boy's real mother is?'

 'Hey, Michael! What's flying like?'

 'Michael, what are you hoping to do now?'

Michael, Sarah and George had to fight their way through the crowd into their house. They were very frightened. The telephone kept ringing, people kept knocking on the front door and some cameramen even went into the back garden and started taking photographs of the house. Sarah closed the curtains. They stood and looked at each other. It was not a happy homecoming• for Michael.

'What shall we do, George?' Sarah asked her husband.

'I don't know,' he answered.

Suddenly there was a very loud knock at the front door and a voice shouted:

'Open the door, please, Mr Broad. Police!'

When George opened it, he saw two tall policemen, a plain clothes inspector• and one of the doctors from the hospital. Other policemen were pushing all the media people back into the street.

George let the inspector and the doctor into the house but the two uniformed policemen stayed outside.

'What you did was very wrong,' the doctor said. 'We told you Michael couldn't go home.'

'But he was tired of being in the hospital,' said Sarah. 'He needs to be at home with us, living a normal life – going to school, playing with his friends…'

'I know, Mrs Broad,' answered the doctor. 'But Michael isn't a normal child. You saw what happened outside. He needs to be protected from the world.'

'But I don't want to live in a hospital for the rest of my life,' shouted Michael. 'I'm not ill. I want to live like other children.'

Glossary

- **homecoming:** time when someone returns home
- **journalists:** people who write stories for newspapers
- **paparazzi:** photographers who take pictures of famous people without their permission
- **plain clothes inspector:** senior police officer not in uniform
- **reporters:** people who write stories for newspapers

'Yes, I know, Michael,' said the doctor. 'But we need to protect you from people like those reporters, and anyone else who might want to use you and hurt you.'

'Hurt him?' asked George. 'But he's just a little boy.'

'Yes, he is,' answered the doctor. 'The only little boy in the world with a pair of wings! We want to make sure that nothing bad happens to him.'

'You just want to keep him in that hospital so that you can study him!' said Sarah. 'You aren't interested in him as a person.'

'In one way you are right, Mrs Broad,' said the doctor. 'Michael is very unusual and scientists from all over the world are interested in his development•. But I can assure you that we *are* concerned• about him as a person.'

The Broads talked to the doctor and the police inspector all evening. Michael went to his bedroom and tried to sleep while plans for his future were made downstairs.

Michael's future

What do you think Michael's parents, the doctor and the police inspector decide?

Imagine you are each of the following people. What do you think is the best for Michael?

- Sarah Broad
- George Broad
- Michael's doctor
- The policeman

Glossary

- **concerned:** worried
- **development:** how he grows, etc.

A change

Early the next morning, Mr Broad walked round to the local newsagent's to buy his morning paper.

'Good morning, John,' he said to the newsagent.

'Morning, George,' the man replied, smiling. 'How does it feel to be famous?'

'What do you mean?' asked George, very surprised.

'Well, look at the front pages of all the papers!' answered the newsagent. 'And I saw you on the TV last night.'

George looked at the national papers on the shelves and saw pictures of himself, his wife and Michael everywhere, and big headlines• that said: MICHAEL FLIES HOME and SUPERBOY HOME AT LAST!

'Michael's a famous star now,' said the newsagent. 'You'll soon be a very rich man, George.'

'Oh, shut up, John!' replied George angrily. 'And give me one copy of all today's papers, please.'

When George got home, the first reporters were already outside the house. They fired• question after question at him:

'What plans have you got for Michael today, Mr Broad?'

'When can we see Michael fly?'

'How does it feel to have such an unusual son?'

George ignored• them.

• **fired:** asked a lot of questions very quickly
• **headlines:** titles of stories in a newspaper

• **ignored:** did not listen to

'Look at this!' he said to Sarah, and put the papers on the kitchen table. 'There are pictures and stories about us everywhere.'

'Oh, no!' she said unhappily.

During breakfast they talked to Michael about the plans for his future.

Later in the morning, two doctors arrived. They took Michael through the crowd of reporters, who were still shouting questions and taking photos, to an ambulance and he was driven back to the hospital.

Michael stayed there for a month. And then, one Monday morning, the police car that Michael was expecting° came to collect him. A policeman put his luggage° in the boot° and then got in the back seat with him. They drove all day, stopping only once for something to eat. At about five o'clock, Michael saw a sign that said 'Scotland', then, an hour or two later, he saw the sea. The car stopped in a lonely place on the coast where a boat was waiting for them. He and the policeman got on it. It was his first time on a boat and he felt quite excited.

Michael was on his way to an island which was an hour's boat-ride from the coast. The name of the island was Shillan. George and Sarah were waiting for him there. They were all very happy as they walked towards the house that was their new home. Inside, the Broads showed Michael around. His bedroom was very big with lovely views of the sea. All his toys and books were already there. For the first time in many months, he felt really happy.

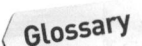

Glossary

- **boot:** space at the back of a car used for carrying things
- **expecting:** waiting for
- **luggage:** bags and cases

Life on Shillan

The next morning at 7.30, Michael's new life began. He got up and had his breakfast in the big warm kitchen with George and Sarah. At 9 o'clock, a doctor called Richard Reed came to the house and took him to a laboratory that was full of special equipment. Dr Reed photographed, weighed• and measured Michael and recorded everything on a computer.

At 9.30, Michael was taken to a room where there were books, paper, paints, tools•, science equipment•, a computer, a TV and DVD player, and a nice big desk.

'This is your classroom,' the doctor said.

Michael sat at the desk and Dr Reed showed him how to switch on the computer.

'Now put on the headset• and go to Channel 10,' said the doctor.

Michael clicked on the Channel 10 icon. Two people sitting at a desk appeared on the screen.

'Good morning, Michael,' they both said.

'My name's Sally Roberts,' said the lady, smiling. 'And this is Paul Brown. We're your teachers. You can use the microphone on your headset to talk to us.'

Glossary

- **equipment:** things you need for a particular job
- **headset:**
- **tools:** instruments for doing work
- **weighed:** measured his weight (kilos, etc.)

30

Every day one or both teachers told him what to do. He did Maths, English, History, and all the other school subjects. He emailed his work to Sally or Paul and they talked about it and helped him if he had problems.

School

What do you study at school?
Are all your subjects compulsory* or can you choose some of them?
Would you like to study like Michael?

At 11.15 he had a drink and some biscuits in the kitchen with Sarah and George. Then he did some more lessons until one o'clock. After lunch, if the weather was good, he went out for a walk.

Michael usually liked going for walks on his own, but sometimes Sarah and George went with him. Twice* a week he had to do a Biology project about the island and send a report* to his teachers the following morning.

Later in the afternoon, Dr Reed returned to the Broads' house and they went to a room where there was a small gym. From four to four thirty every day Michael had to do exercises, which Dr Reed filmed. Sometimes they were exercises like all children do at school, but other times the doctor made him do special exercises to make his wings and chest muscles strong.

In the evenings he played computer games, watched TV, played cards or other games with Sarah and George, or read books from the library in the classroom.

- **compulsory:** that you must do
- **report:** description of what is done or said

- **twice:** two times

Shillan was a small island. At the southern end there was a little harbour• where boats arrived. The cottage where Dr Reed lived was there, too. Michael's house was in the east of the island. Behind the house there was a wood of pine trees• called Laird's Wood and a lake called Goose Loch. In winter many ducks and geese• came to swim and feed• on the lake. The southern part of Shillan was quite flat and covered with grass, but the north was hilly. In the northwest there were two hills: Castle Hill, which got its name from a ruined castle that stood on the top it, and Crag Hill, which was very rocky. Lots of wild flowers grew on the island – some of them were quite rare.

Glossary

- **feed:** eat; get food
- **geese:**
- **harbour:** port
- **missed:** sad because they weren't there
- **pine trees:**

Soon Michael knew every centimetre of the island and he could recognise most of the flowers, birds and animals that lived there. At first he missed• the company of other children, but as time passed he got used to playing by himself.

Sarah and George loved their new life. They no longer had to work in the shop and had time for their hobbies. George grew vegetables in the garden and Sarah painted pictures of wild flowers. When she wasn't painting or doing housework, she made clothes for Michael. Sarah designed an extra-large jacket for him, which was easy to put on and which covered his wings.

And sometimes Michael flew. He could fly from his house to the north end of the island in fifteen minutes. As he got better at it, he flew higher and for a longer time. One Saturday when he was eight years old he came home at lunchtime and said, 'Guess what, George! I flew all round the coast of the island this morning! I had to stop four times, but not for very long.' George and Sarah were surprised, but then they realised that Michael's flight was only like a long bicycle ride or a game of football for other children.

And so the days passed happily for the Broads and Michael. Once a month a boat came and brought them food and any other supplies[•] they needed. Otherwise[•] they saw nobody else. They watched the seasons come and go. In winter the sea was very rough[•] and sometimes frightening, and it usually snowed several[•] times. In summer the weather was often very beautiful and the days were long – it was light enough to see until ten o'clock at night.

Michael grew stronger and taller. He worked hard at his lessons and became a very clever boy. George and Sarah were pleased with their decision to move to Shillan because Michael was able to grow up out of the public eye[•].

Your home

Where do you live? Tick (✔).

☐ In a big city ☐ In a small town or village
☐ In a town ☐ In the country

With a partner discuss the advantages and disadvantages of where you live.

A plan

One evening, when Michael was twelve years old, Dr Reed came to see them. He wanted to talk about something.

'I got a phone call from my boss in London,' he said. 'The BBC have asked if they can make a film about Michael.'

Sarah looked worried. She still had bad memories of reporters, photographers and television crews*.

'I'm not sure it's a very good idea,' she said.

'Wait a minute, Sarah,' said George. 'Let's listen to what the doctor says. Go on, Richard.'

'The producer of *Strange But True* wants to include a 45-minute documentary about Michael in his new series,' Dr Reed explained. 'My boss thinks that it might be a good idea. Michael's growing up. We can't keep him on this island forever. We need to introduce the people of Britain to him so that one day he can live a normal life somewhere – go to university, get a job and so on.'

'Well, I agree with that,' said George. 'But isn't it dangerous for him now? He's still young, after all.'

'I'd like to do it,' said Michael. 'We've seen every episode of *Strange But True* on TV. It's a great programme.'

Television

Do you like watching television?
What are your favourite television programmes?
Do you want to be on television?
Do you think Michael is making the correct decision?

'Yes, it is,' agreed the doctor. 'The producers of the programme are very serious people. Naturally, we'll see the film before it goes on television to make sure it's alright.'

'They can't make the film here, though. It's too dangerous,' said Sarah. 'Someone might recognise the place, and then all those newspaper reporters will come here.'

'Yes, obviously they must make it somewhere else,' said Dr Reed.

'Well, I'm still not sure it's a good idea,' said Sarah, looking at George.

'Do you think it's too risky• for Michael, Richard?' asked George.

'No, I don't,' said Dr Reed. 'And there's another point. Quite an important one. The BBC will give Michael £10,000 if we let them make the film.'

'Wow!' said Michael. 'That means I could buy… I could buy… anything!'

'Well, actually,' said the doctor laughing. 'It isn't a bad idea for Michael to have some money in the bank for the future.'

'Yes, you're right,' said Sarah.

'So, shall I tell my boss to go ahead and make the arrangements?' asked Dr Reed.

The Broads looked at Michael, and then at each other. They all nodded• their heads.

'Right! I'll talk to him tomorrow,' said the doctor. 'And now, what about a game of cards?'

Glossary

- **nodded:** moved their heads up and down to mean 'yes'
- **risky:** that might be dangerous or hurt him
- **television crews:** groups of people who make a television programme

The film

A police helicopter flew in to pick them up• one morning in May. Sarah, George, Michael and Dr Reed were waiting for it in the field. They all climbed inside and it took off•. It was a beautiful day and the views of the mountains, lakes and river valleys were wonderful. At midday the helicopter landed at a deserted• airport.

'This was an important military centre, but it's not used now,' explained Dr. Reed as they walked over to some buildings. 'My boss chose it because it's a long way from Shillan and there are no people around. Also, they can film Michael flying inside the big hangars• where they kept the planes years ago.'

The people from the BBC were already there. Dr Reed introduced everyone and then the producer of *Strange But True*, Paul Salter, invited them to have some lunch together.

'We want to film some interviews with you all,' said Paul. 'There are only four of us here – Mary, who will interview you, Steve, our cameraman•, Jeff, the sound and lighting• technician, and myself. We want everyone to be as relaxed as possible, so we'll do all the interviews here in this room. Later on we'll move into a hangar to film Michael flying.'

After lunch the BBC people set up• their equipment. Just before they went to do the first interviews, Dr Reed turned to George, Sarah and Michael. 'Remember! Do *not* mention Shillan! Don't even say we live on an island, or that we live in Scotland. We don't want the BBC people to know where we live. OK?'

Glossary

- **cameraman:** person who films
- **deserted:** place with no people in it
- **hangars:** large buildings where planes are kept
- **lighting:** how lights are used in a film
- **pick them up:** get them
- **set up:** got ready (to start working)
- **took off:** went up in the air

George, Sarah and Michael nodded.

During the next two days the four of them were interviewed alone, in pairs and as a group. Then, at lunchtime on the third day, Paul Salter called them all together.

'Thank you all very much,' he said. 'We've got some great interviews on film now so you can all take this afternoon off•. Tomorrow morning we'll go to the hangar to get some pictures of Michael in the air.'

The interview

With a partner think of questions to ask Michael.
Share them with the class and choose the best five.
Then with your partner take turns being Michael
and the interviewer and answer all of the questions.
Act out the interviews in class.

That afternoon, when the Broads were having a rest and Dr Reed was talking to Paul Salter, Michael went out for a walk. He walked over to have a closer look at the helicopter when he heard footsteps• behind him. It was Jeff.

'Hey, Mickey!' he said. 'What are you doing?'

'Just having a look at this helicopter,' answered Michael coldly. He didn't like being called Mickey.

'Have you seen the old planes?' Jeff was trying to be friendly.

'What planes?'

'There are some old warplanes• here,' Jeff said. 'Would you like to see them?'

'Yes, OK,' said Michael. 'Where are they?'

'In Number 2 hangar,' replied Jeff. 'Did you enjoy doing the interviews, Mickey?'

'Well,' said Michael. 'It was alright at first, but then it got a bit boring.'

'I expect you're looking forward to tomorrow,' said the technician.

'Why?' asked Michael, puzzled•.

'Well, you're flying tomorrow, aren't you? It's really amazing.'

'Well, I suppose it is,' said Michael. 'For other people.'

'What do the kids at your school say?' asked Jeff, looking at Michael with a strange expression on his face.

'They don't say anything,' answered Michael.

'Why's that?'

'Well, there isn't a school on Shill…,' Michael stopped himself before he said all of the name.

'Shill? Where's that?' asked Jeff. 'I've never heard of anywhere called Shill.'

'Er – it's – er – it's…,' said Michael, going very red in the face. 'Um – I have to get back now, Jeff. It's getting late.'

And he turned round and ran off leaving the technician looking at him. 'On Shill,' he said to himself. 'Hmm… on Shill…'

The filming of Michael flying in the hangar went very well. They finished in time for lunch, and at seven o'clock that evening the Broads, Michael and Dr Reed were back on the island of Shillan.

• **puzzled:** confused

• **warplanes:** airplanes used in war/for fighting

Jeff's Friends

The phone rang in Slim Wilson's study. He switched off the TV and went to answer it.

'Slim?'

'Yes?'

'It's Jeff. Jeff Hunter.'

'Hello Jeff. Any news?'

'Yes, I think I've found something out. Can I come round?'

'OK. Come at 7.30. Peters will be here.'

Jeff rang the doorbell and Wilson let him in. Peters, a large, bald-headed• man, was sitting on the sofa.

'Well?' asked Wilson.

'The boy is amazing, Slim,' Jeff said. 'He's exactly what we need for the job. One minute he's standing on the ground, then he moves those wings of his, and up he goes! It's incredible!'

'Did you find out where he lives?' asked Peters.

'Well, it wasn't easy,' Jeff replied. 'They were extremely careful. But I talked to the boy alone one day. He started to say a name, then stopped.'

'What did he say?' asked Wilson.

'He said "There isn't a school on Shill".'

'Where's Shill?' asked Wilson.

'I don't know. I asked him, but he didn't tell me,' said Jeff. 'When I got home, I looked at a map but I couldn't find it.'

Wilson went over to his bookcase and took out a big atlas with detailed maps of Britain in it. He looked in the index.

Glossary

- **bald-headed:** with no hair on his head

'There's nowhere called Shill in Britain,' he said. 'Perhaps they live in another country.'

'Maybe, but I think it was just the first part of a longer name,' said Jeff. Wilson looked at the index again. 'Shilbottle, Shildon, Shillan, three Shillfords, Shillingstone…,' he read. 'There are lots of places beginning with Shill.'

'Well, let's see where they are on the maps,' said Jeff. 'It can't be a town or a city. It must be somewhere small.'

The three men checked all the places on the maps and discussed those that seemed possible.

'Shillmoor is in the hills in the north of England,' said Jeff. 'It must be very small because it isn't on my map at home.'

'Yes, it's just two or three houses. Look.' said Peters, pointing to the map.

'And Shiltenish seems even smaller,' said Jeff. 'It's in Scotland, miles from anywhere. And then there's Shillan – an island near the west coast of Scotland.'

'What do you think, Slim?' said Peters.

'Tell me what the boy said again, Jeff,' said Wilson.

'He said, "There isn't a school on Shill…",' Jeff answered.

'Well, there's the answer!' said Wilson, smiling.

Jeff and Peters looked puzzled.

The place

How does Wilson know that Michael is on Shillan?

What clue does Jeff give him that tells him?

'What do you mean?' asked Peters.

'The boy said, 'There isn't a school *on* Shill…',' Wilson explained. ' *On* Shill… . Not *in* Shill. You only say *on* when you're talking about a hill or an island. Shillmoor is a village on a hill, not a hill itself. Shiltenish is on an island, not an island itself. Shillan is the name of an island. 'There's no school on *Shillan*.' That's what Michael *didn't* say!'

The other two men looked at Wilson.

'Congratulations, Sherlock Holmes!' said Peters, and they all laughed.

On an island

Michael lives *on* an island.

Complete the following sentences with the correct prepositions.

a)   Diana wants to live …………………………………… London.

b)   My house is …………………………………… the corner of the road.

c)   He is waiting …………………………………… the bus stop.

d)   My mum is …………………………………… home.

e)   York is …………………………………… the north of England.

f)   We are going …………………………………… holidays next week.

g)   Their new house is …………………………………… the centre.

h)   We had a picnic …………………………………… that mountain.

Visitors on Shillan

After the filming trip, life on Shillan returned to normal. A few weeks later a copy of the documentary arrived from the BBC. The doctor and the Broads sat down to watch it that same evening. They found it very strange to see themselves on film.

'Well done, everybody!' said Dr Reed. 'We managed to do all the interviews without saying where we lived. I'll talk to my boss tomorrow and tell him we're happy for the BBC to show the film on television.'

That night three men landed on Shillan's East Beach in a small rubber dinghy. They hid it behind some rocks and covered it with pieces of wood that they found on the beach.

They looked at their map with a torch.

'Right,' said Wilson. 'We need to go north.'

Jeff Hunter looked at his compass[•]. 'This way,' he said.

They walked along the path until they came to Crag Hill, then they went west to Castle Hill.

'OK,' said Wilson. 'This is the place!'

They walked silently up the side of the hill. It was just starting to get light when they got to the ruined castle on the top.

'This is a very good place,' said Peters, looking over the wall. 'We'll be able to see everything from here.'

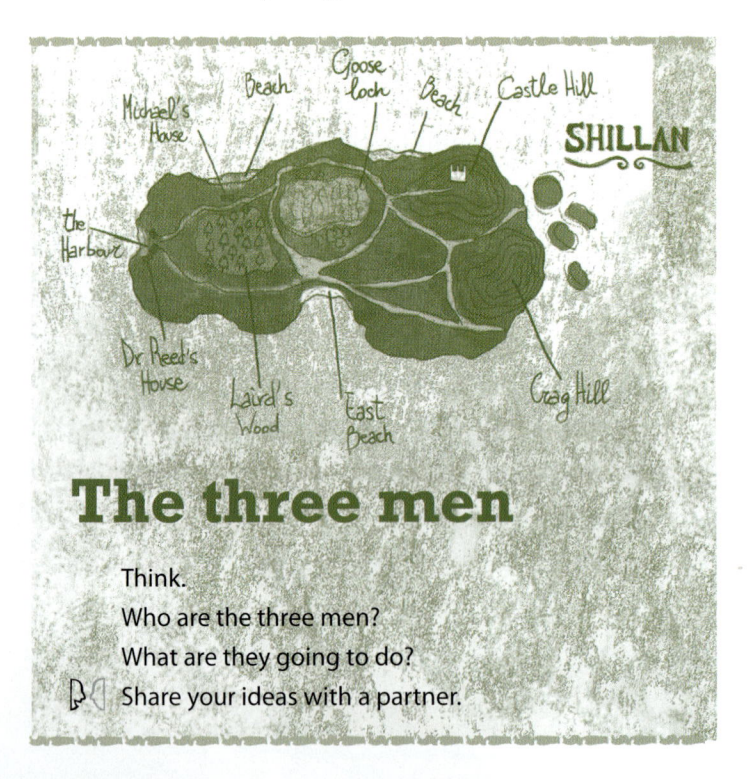

The three men

Think.

Who are the three men?

What are they going to do?

Share your ideas with a partner.

 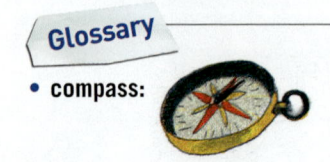

After his morning lessons Michael went down into the kitchen for lunch. Sarah was taking a fish pie out of the oven.

'Dr Reed caught the fish yesterday,' she said. 'Go and call George, please!'

After lunch, Michael got up and gave Sarah a big hug•. 'That was delicious•!' he said. 'My compliments to the chef•!' Sarah laughed.

'I'm off to do my Biology homework now. See you later. Bye!' And he picked up his rucksack and went out into the warm sunshine.

He took the path to Goose Loch. He was doing a project on the plants that were growing in the wet grass around the lake. There were some rare species, and he was making a map of where they grew.

- **my compliments to the chef:** way of thanking someone for a good meal
- **delicious:** good (of food)
- **hug:** when you put your arms around someone

'There he is!' said Jeff to Wilson.

'He's walking along the path, next to the lake. Look!'

Wilson took the binoculars• and looked through them. He watched Michael walk to the northern end of Goose Loch.

'He's stopped,' Wilson said. 'He's taking out a book and he's writing something.'

'What do you think he's doing?' asked Peters.

'I don't know,' answered Wilson. 'I think he's making notes about something he's seen in the grass.'

They watched for a bit longer. Michael continued to write.

Suddenly Jeff said, 'OK! Are you ready?'

'Yes,' said Wilson. 'Peters, have you got the gun?'

'Yes. Here it is!' answered Peters.

'OK. Pick up your stuff• and let's go!'

The three men crept• quietly down the side of Castle Hill and across the grass towards Michael. When they were about 200 metres away from him, they stopped and lay down on the ground on their stomachs. Peters got his gun ready. They waited.

After a while•, Michael put his book in his rucksack and stood up. Peters aimed• and fired. Michael shouted with pain, then fell down. The three men got up and ran to where the boy lay. Peters pulled a small dart• out of Michael's left arm and then helped Jeff to lift the boy up. They carried him round the lake to Laird's Wood.

They had to find somewhere to hide until it got dark, and the wood was ideal. They walked until they came to a small grassy space in the thickest• part of the wood.

Glossary

- **aimed:** pointed a gun
- **binoculars:**
- **crept:** moved very quietly and slowly
- **dart:**
- **stuff:** things
- **thickest:** with most trees
- **while:** short period of time

They lay Michael's unconscious* body on the ground and then sat down next to him.

'When do you think it'll be safe to leave, Slim?' asked Jeff.

'I think we'll have to wait until at least 9 o'clock,' said Wilson. 'It gets dark so late here in the north in the summer.'

'So we'll have to stay here for about six hours,' said Jeff.

'Yes,' replied Wilson. 'The boat's coming back to pick us up at 10 o'clock. How long does the effect of the sleeping drug* last, Peters?'

'Twelve hours,' Peters answered.

'Good!' said Wilson. 'We'll just have to sit here and wait. Let's hope nobody starts looking for him.'

What happens next?

What do you think happens next?
Choose from the situations below.

- ☐ Michael wakes up before they leave and escapes from the three men.
- ☐ The three men kidnap* Michael and ask for a ransom* from George and Sarah.
- ☐ The three men want Michael to steal* something for them.
- ☐ The three men want Michael to teach them to fly.
- ☐ One of the three men is Michael's real father and he wants to see him.

Then continue the story for that situation.

Glossary

- **drug:** medicine
- **kidnap:** take a person and ask for money (or another thing) in exchange for giving him/her back safely
- **ransom:** money you pay when someone is kidnapped
- **steal:** take something that doesn't belong to you
- **unconscious:** not awake

Michael is Missing

At ten to four Sarah started to get the tea ready. She made a pot● of tea and put some cakes on the table. Michael always came home hungry and thirsty after his afternoon walks. At four o'clock Dr Reed arrived to join them.

'It's a beautiful day, Sarah,' he said when she let him into the kitchen. 'One of the best we've had this summer.'

'Yes, it is,' said the Sarah. 'Sit down, Richard. Michael will be home soon. I'll go and call George. He's still working in the vegetable garden.'

'Well, actually, Sarah,' said the doctor. 'He's fast asleep● in a garden chair in the sun.'

They both laughed as Sarah poured● the tea.

They drank tea, ate cakes and talked while they waited. At half past four Sarah stood up and went over to the window.

'It's not like Michael to be so late,' she said.

'Oh, don't worry, Sarah,' said Dr Reed. 'Where's he gone?'

'I don't know,' she answered. 'He had some homework to do.'

They waited for another fifteen minutes, then George came in.

'Hello, Richard,' he said. 'Is there any tea left, Sarah love?'

'Michael hasn't come back yet, George,' said Sarah.

'Hasn't he?' answered her husband. 'I expect he's still watching the birds.'

'I'll just go and check his computer and find out what his homework was today,' said Dr Reed, and went upstairs. A few minutes later he came back into the kitchen.

● **fast asleep:** in a deep sleep
● **pot:**

● **poured:** put liquid into a cup, glass or bottle

'He's studying the plants at the north end of Goose Loch,' he said. 'I'll walk up there and see what he's doing.'

It took Richard Reed twenty minutes to get to the lake. He looked all around and shouted 'Michael!' two or three times. But there was no answer. The doctor was puzzled. This was not like Michael. He was hardly ever• late for meals. Tea was always at four o'clock. Now it was half past five.

'Did you hear that?' said Jeff.
'What?' asked Wilson, sitting up.
'Listen!' answered Jeff.
They heard a man's voice shouting, 'Michael!'
'That's the doctor,' said Jeff. 'Dr Reed.'
They sat very quietly and listened. The doctor called twice more.

Dr Reed went back to the house, hoping to find Michael there. But only Sarah and George were in the kitchen. Sarah began to cry.

'Don't worry, love,' George said, putting his arm around her. 'He'll soon be home. He's probably found something interesting to do and has forgotten the time.'

But secretly he was worried too. Michael was always very reliable•.

'I'm going to walk up to the top of Castle Hill,' said Dr Reed. 'I'll be able to see him from there. Can I borrow• your binoculars, George?'

'Certainly!' he answered. 'Wait! I'll come with you.'

The two men set off along the track•. They walked quickly. It was now seven o'clock but it was still sunny and warm. Occasionally• one of them shouted 'Michael!', but apart from that, neither of them said anything as they walked along.

Glossary

- **borrow:** take something from someone for a period of time
- **hardly ever:** not very often
- **occasionally:** from time to time
- **reliable:** that you can trust
- **track:** path

The prisoner

When Michael woke up, he found himself in a small, dark place. He was inside a box and his hands were tied together behind his back. He knew that he must be in a car or a van because he was thrown to one side when the vehicle went round a corner. For a moment he felt confused, but then his mind started to clear.

'I remember that I was studying flowers and suddenly I felt a pain in my arm. Then everything went dark. But where am I now? How did I get here? And where am I going?'

After what seemed like a long time, the car or van stopped and he heard voices.

'Help!' he shouted as loudly as he could. 'Help me!'

Slim Wilson looked at Jeff and Peters nervously.

'He's woken up,' said Wilson. 'Let's get him inside quickly.'

Peters unlocked the back doors of the van and together the three men lifted out a large box. There were several similar• boxes in the van.

'Let me out!' shouted Michael. But the three men took no notice. They carried the box into a small room inside a building and put it on the floor.

'Now listen carefully, Michael,' said Wilson, putting his face very close to the box. 'We've got a job for you to do, and if you do it well, we'll let you go. But if you don't, we'll kill• Sarah Broad. She's here too, in another room here. Do you understand?'

'Yes,' said Michael. 'I understand. But let me out of here. I'm thirsty.'

Wilson made a sign to Peters and Hunter. They opened the box, pulled Michael out and put him on a chair. When he saw the men, Michael felt really scared. They were all wearing balaclavas over their faces. One of them was holding a bottle of water.

'Please untie• my hands,' said Michael.

'Only if you promise to be good,' said Wilson. 'Remember what I said about Sarah.'

'I'll be good,' said Michael.

Wilson nodded and Peters cut the rope. Michael took the water and drank. Then, before Wilson knew what was happening, Michael threw the bottle at him, jumped up, opened his wings and flew up to the ceiling.

Glossary

- **kill:** stop someone from living
- **similar:** that are like other ones; almost the same
- **untie:** open a knot; free a cord or rope

'Get him down!' shouted Wilson.

The three men tried to catch the boy as he circled• the room. In the end Peters climbed onto the table, took hold of Michael's leg and pulled him down.

'If you do that again,' shouted Wilson angrily, 'Sarah will die! Tie his wings so that he can't fly!'

Peters and Hunter got some rope• and tied it tightly• around Michael's wings and body.

'Now, listen!' said Wilson. 'I'll repeat what I said before. We want you to do a simple job for us, and then we'll let you go. We don't want to hurt you, and we don't want to hurt your mum. OK? If you do what we say, everything will be fine. Are you going to be a good boy?'

Michael nodded.

Michael

How do you think Michael feels?
Close your eyes and imagine
you are Michael.
Then describe how you feel.
Think of the following.

- Where are you?
- Are you afraid?
- Have you got any pains?
- Who are the men?
- What are they going to ask you to do?

Glossary

- **circled:** went in circles
- **rope:**

- **tightly:** firmly; strongly

Wilson looked at Jeff. 'Now give him some food before we tell him what he has to do.'

Jeff gave Michael some sandwiches. Jeff didn't speak, but Michael was sure that he knew this man. There was something familiar° about the way he moved. A little later, he took Michael into another room where there was a computer.

'Sit down, Michael, and watch this piece of film,' said Wilson.

Michael watched. He saw a high wall with guards standing along it every few hundred metres. Then he saw the wall from the air. It surrounded° a group of buildings. The camera zoomed in on some of them – they looked like offices.

'Now, Michael,' said Wilson. 'Inside that building there is something that I want very much. And that's why I need your help. I want you to fly over the wall. And get something for me inside. Now come here and look at these plans°.'

He took Michael to a large table in the corner where there were plans of the building.

'This is the building you have to go into,' said Wilson, pointing to a red square on the first plan. 'And this is what it looks like inside.' He showed Michael a plan of a room. 'You have to go into this room, open this cupboard and take out an envelope with the word "Lion" written on the front.'

During the following two hours, Wilson gave Michael detailed instructions about what he had to do.

- **familiar:** that you know
- **plans:** maps of the rooms in a building

- **surrounded:** was around

The search begins

Back on Shillan, the Broads and Dr Reed called the police. The police arrived by helicopter and started to search the area. The following morning the search party* found footprints* on the sand at East Beach and the marks left by a rubber dinghy.

Just before midday, Detective Riley went to the Broads' house to give them an up-to-date report.

'So now we know he isn't on the island,' he said. 'And that he was taken away in a rubber dinghy.'

'Please find him soon!' sobbed* Sarah.

'We will, Mrs Broad. Don't worry!' said Riley gently. 'We have some of our best people working on it right now.'

'Have you got any ideas about who's kidnapped him?' asked George.

'A few,' Riley answered. 'The only people you've been in contact with are the four from the BBC. We've already spoken to three of them, but we can't find Hunter.'

'Jeff?' asked Dr Reed.

'Yes, the technician,' said the detective.

'So what can we do?' asked George.

'Nothing at the moment, I'm afraid,' replied Riley. 'But if it's any comfort to you, we're giving this case* top priority*.'

Glossary

- **case:** when police investigate something
- **footprints:** marks made by feet
- **search party:** group of people looking for someone
- **sobbed:** cried noisily, taking short breaths
- **top priority:** great importance

Breaking in

The next morning, Peters dyed• Michael's beautiful white feathers black.

'To make you more difficult to see at night!'

While they dried, Wilson put a belt around Michael's waist and fitted• two electronic gadgets• to it. One was a transmitter• he could use to talk to Wilson. The other was an explosive device•.

'If you do anything wrong, Michael, this device• will explode and that will be the end of you! And the end of Sarah Broad!' Wilson said. Then he gave Michael a microphone and headphones to use with the transmitter. Wilson told him to practise talking to Peters in the next room so that they could check• the system.

Around three o'clock, Michael had to put on a black jacket, black trousers and a black balaclava. He was now certain that one of the men was Jeff from the BBC, even though he never spoke and the others never used his name.

At five o'clock, the gang, with Michael, set off for the Government Nuclear Research Complex•. They made Michael get back into the box and then put the box back into the van. Michael's wings were still tied and he was very uncomfortable. They drove for about four hours and he was very happy when the van finally stopped and the men let him out.

Glossary

- **check:** control; make sure it works
- **complex:** number of buildings in one structure
- **device:** machine used to do a specific thing
- **dyed:** changed the colour of
- **explosive device:** bomb
- **fitted:** attached; put
- **gadgets:** technical machines or equipment
- **transmitter:** machine used for sending signals

'There's the complex,' said Wilson, pointing to a wall with some floodlights• on the top. 'Now, Michael! You know what you have to do, and you know what will happen if you do anything different, don't you?'

'Yes,' said Michael. 'I know.' He was scared but he didn't show it. He didn't want to help these criminals steal secret documents from this government building. And he didn't want to be discovered and shot by the guards.

'Good,' said Wilson. 'OK, you two! Untie his wings!'

When Hunter and Peters took off the rope, Michael opened and closed his wings a few times. Wilson checked his watch.

'Right, a quarter to ten,' he said. 'We have fifteen minutes before they change the guards and you go in, Michael. Let's check the electrical equipment.'

Jeff came and switched on the various gadgets attached to Michael's belt, and then he checked Wilson and Peters' monitors. They all tested their microphones and headphones to see if they were working correctly.

'Thanks, Jeff,' said Michael quietly when Peters and Wilson were talking together a few metres away.

'That's OK... Huh? What did you say?' asked Hunter with a surprised look on his face

'I said, "Thanks, Jeff",' replied Michael.

'How did you... er... My name isn't Jeff. It's... er... it's... Steve,' replied Hunter, not very convincingly.

'Oh, sorry – Steve!' said Michael. 'You remind• me of someone I know.'

'Are we ready, then?' asked Wilson, walking over to Michael and Hunter.

Glossary

- **floodlights:** very strong lights used for lighting public buildings
- **you remind me:** (here) you are like

'Yes. Everything's working perfectly,' answered Jeff.
'Good,' said Wilson. 'It's time to go then, Michael.'

Michael took off and flew high into the sky. He flew in large circles above the three men. Up, up, up! Soon he was above the beams• of the floodlights. As he hovered• in the air, he thought about landing in the courtyard• and telling the guards the truth. 'A gang of criminals has kidnapped me and they want me to steal something very important from here. Help me, please!' But no, he couldn't do that. The criminals were following all his moves• on their transmitters. So, what could he do? He thought and thought but he didn't have an answer to that question. He decided to wait and see what happened inside the building.

- **beams:** lines of light
- **courtyard:** square area surrounded by buildings
- **hovered:** kept in the same position in the air
- **moves:** actions; movements

'Any news?' asked George as Riley came back into the living room after a long phone conversation. It was four o'clock in the afternoon. Hundreds of miles away, the criminals were getting ready to set off• for the Nuclear Complex.

'Yes, there is,' said the detective. 'Our people have searched Hunter's flat• and checked his emails. In his emails he talks about an "objective•" in the north of England. He also adds that it is "remote•". We think that the people who have taken Michael want to use him to fly into a place which is surrounded by a high wall or something similar. We have found four places like this in the north of England and we're sending officers to each of those now. We have also located the house of the person that Hunter was emailing.'

Email

Do you use email?

Have you got your own email address?

Who do you send emails to?

Which of the following do you use? Tick (✔).

☐ A social network   ☐ A photo-sharing network

☐ A chat programme   ☐ A music-sharing network

☐ A blog

🗣 Share the results in class.

Glossary

- **flat:** apartment
- **objective:** thing you want
- **remote:** far from other buildings or people
- **set off:** start a journey

'But there's no news of Michael?' asked Sarah.

'I'm afraid not,' answered Riley. 'But we're getting closer every minute.'

Just then, Riley's mobile phone rang. 'Excuse me,' he said and he went outside. Five minutes later he came back in with a strange expression on his face.

'Good news?' asked George. 'Or bad news?'

'Well both, actually,' replied Riley. 'Hunter was emailing a man called Edward Wilson, known as "Slim". That's the good news because now we know who we're looking for.'

'And the bad news?' asked George.

'Wilson is a well-known international criminal•. We've examined his computer and discovered that he is working with an important terrorist group. The "objective" in the north of England is something that the terrorists want. And they'll pay a lot of money for it.'

'Oh dear,' said George. 'And Michael is involved too, now.'

'Yes,' said Riley. 'However, it makes the possible site easier to identify. We think they're going to break into• either the Warefield Military Weapons• Establishment• near York or the Government Nuclear Research Complex outside Leeds. So we're sending most of our men to those two sites. The employees at both places have been told to continue working normally so that the criminals don't become suspicious•. We need to catch Wilson and stop him from selling any more government secrets to terrorist groups.'

'But what about Michael?' asked Sarah tearfully•.

'He'll be alright, Mrs Broad,' said Riley kindly. 'We'll make sure of that!'

Glossary

- **break into:** enter illegally
- **criminal:** person who breaks the law, does illegal things
- **establishment:** building
- **suspicious:** (here) think that the police know what they are doing
- **tearfully:** with tears in her eyes
- **weapons:** guns, etc.

Michael flies in

When he was high enough, Michael looked down. He could see the van parked among the trees, but he couldn't see the gang. He started to fly towards the wall. He went through the details of the plan in his head. He had to wait until he heard the bell ring at ten o'clock. It took fifteen minutes for the guards to change. During those fifteen minutes there was nobody outside the building. That was when he had to fly in.

He dropped a little lower in the sky and hovered there, waiting. A minute later the bell rang and he saw the guards start to move away from their posts•. He flew quickly over the wall and dropped down to the ground next to the building he had to enter. There was a sign saying 'Head Office' on it. He spoke quietly into his microphone.

'I'm outside the building.'

'Right.' *(Wilson's voice.)* 'Walk round to the main• door.'

The lights were very bright in the courtyard. Michael was shaking all over. 'Someone's sure to see me,' he thought.

'I'm at the main door.'

'OK. Now press these keys on the number pad• on the door. Ready? 7-8-5-0-7-9-9.'

'OK. Done.'

'Now press the key that says "Enter".'

Michael pressed the 'Enter' key. He heard a click.

'The door's open.'

'Good. Now go and do everything I told you to do. Call me again when you get out with the "Lion" envelope.'

Glossary

- **main**: most important
- **number pad:**
- **posts**: positions
- **sensors**: instruments that react to certain physical conditions; alarms

Michael knew that, once inside, he had to fly up to the ceiling of the corridor in front of him. The office he had to go to was at the end of this corridor. He had to fly because there were electronic sensors• connected to the alarm system in the lower part of the walls of the corridor.

He slowly pushed the door open. To his amazement, he saw a man in military uniform standing in the middle of the corridor. He was holding a large sign which said:

MICHAEL, DON'T SPEAK!

IT'S OK.

THE POLICE ARE HERE.

YOU CAN WALK TO THE OFFICE.

THE ALARMS ARE OFF.

The man smiled, and Michael smiled back. He walked down the corridor to the office, where there was a uniformed• policeman. He held a sign which said:

MICHAEL, DON'T SAY ANYTHING!
TAKE THE ENVELOPE OUT OF THE CUPBOARD.
THERE'S A TRACKING DEVICE• IN IT.
THERE'S ANOTHER TRACKING DEVICE ON THE DESK.
PUT IT IN YOUR POCKET.

Michael found the envelope and put it in his pocket, together with the tracking device. He waved• cheerily• at the policeman and walked out of the office and down the corridor. For the first time in two days, he didn't feel so frightened. As he stepped out into the courtyard, two more policemen smiled and gave him the thumbs up sign•. He spoke into his microphone, 'I've got the "Lion" envelope.'

'Good!' said Wilson. 'Now fly straight back to us.'

He flapped• his wings and flew up high to get above the lights. He knew that he had to follow the plan so as not to make the men suspicious. As he flew over the wall, he started to feel scared again.

 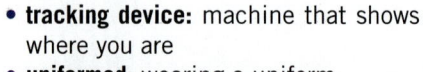

Good news on Shillan

'We've found him!' said Detective Riley to the Broads as he came back into the living room after his latest phone call.

'Oh, that's wonderful news!' said Sarah. 'Where is he now?'

'He's still with the criminals,' answered Riley. 'But our officers have given him a tracking device so we can follow him everywhere he goes.'

'But why is he back with the criminals?' asked Sarah. 'Isn't that dangerous?'

'We need to catch these people, Mrs Broad,' said Detective Riley, 'And we think that they will lead• us to the terrorists. We can't rescue Michael yet. We need him.'

'Oh, dear!' said Sarah. 'So he's not safe at all. You're going to use him to find those terrible people.'

'I'm sorry, Mrs Broad,' answered Riley. 'But you must understand that I'm doing this for the safety of the country, and perhaps the whole world. We have to catch these people now.'

Detective Riley

Do you think Detective Riley did the correct thing?
What does Sarah think?

 Imagine you are Detective Riley.
Explain your plans to a partner.

• lead: take

The Appointment

🎧 ¹⁷ Michael flew back to where the three men were hiding.

'Here it is!' he said, handing over the "Lion" envelope.

'Good boy!' said Wilson, smiling. 'You've done a great job.' Then he turned to Peters and Hunter. 'And now, gentlemen! Let's go and meet our friends!'

'What about the boy?' asked Peters.

'We'll take him with us, just in case•,' replied Wilson. 'Tie him up!' said Wilson. 'And take off the belt, microphone and headphones, too! Then put him back in the box. I'm not taking any chances. The whole country's probably looking for him now. And change into your normal clothes as soon as you've put him into the van.'

Jeff Hunter dug• a hole in the ground and buried• their black

Glossary

- **buried:** put something in a hole in the ground and covered it
- **dug:** made a hole in the ground
- **just in case:** if he is needed
- **plenty:** lots
- **staring:** looking in a fixed way

68

clothes and balaclavas. Then they got in the van.

'Where to, Slim?' asked Peters, who was driving.

'Drive south!' answered Wilson. 'Follow the signs for the M62 motorway, then go west. We're heading for Manchester Airport. I have an appointment with our clients at six o'clock tomorrow morning so we've got plenty• of time. Drive slowly and carefully. I'm going to have a little sleep now. Wake me up when we're ten miles from the airport.'

They got to the motorway just after midnight. Wilson was still asleep. Hunter was staring• out of the window. He was worried. Did Michael really know who he was? Peters was thinking about his share of the payment – a million pounds! Neither of them noticed that two dark blue cars were following them. They didn't hear the helicopter flying above them either.

When they were ten miles from the airport, Peters said: 'Wake up, Slim! We're nearly there.'

Wilson yawned• and stretched•. He looked at the road signs on the motorway. 'OK, Peters,' he said. 'We're not actually going to the airport. I'm meeting my clients at the Grand Hotel. You'll see a sign for it soon.'

About three miles from the airport, they turned off and drove through an area with hotels, car parks and warehouses•.

'There it is!' said Hunter, pointing to a large square building with the name 'Grand Hotel' in bright neon lights on the roof.

'Right,' said Wilson. 'Drive into the car park, Peters, and find somewhere quiet to park. Not too far away. I want to be able to see the entrance.'

Peters parked and Slim Wilson looked at his watch. 'Good,' he said. 'Almost three o'clock. I booked a room here last week so I'll just go up and have a shower and make myself smart before my clients arrive. You two can stay in the van. But keep your eyes open. Peters, get your gun ready just in case something goes wrong. We'll meet again when I've done the deal•.'

He took his briefcase• containing the "Lion" envelope and walked across the car park and through the glass doors of the hotel.

At the same time as Wilson went to have his shower, two dark blue cars entered the hotel car park. One of them parked opposite the entrance and the other one parked opposite the van.

Glossary

- **briefcase:** small case for documents, etc.
- **deal:** business agreement
- **stretched:** made his arms and legs as long as possible
- **warehouses:** big buildings where materials or goods are kept
- **yawned:** opened his mouth wide because he was sleepy

At five o'clock, while Peters and Hunter were dozing• in their van, a large white van with 'Conference Logistics' written on its side parked immediately outside the hotel entrance. A lot of men dressed in white overalls• climbed out and opened the back doors. They unloaded• lots of boards and signs and other equipment and carried everything into the lobby• of the hotel.

'What's going on?' asked Peters, waking up suddenly.

Hunter yawned. 'Oh, it looks like there's a conference at the hotel today,' he said. 'Look at the banner• that they're putting up above the entrance. It says *3rd National Conference: Surgery Today*. It must be an event for doctors. They often have them at these hotels.'

The men in the van

Who do you think the men in the white van are? Tick (✔).

☐ They are helpers at the conference.
☐ They are policemen.
☐ They are terrorists.

What happens next?

- **banner:** long piece of cloth with writing on it
- **dozing:** sleeping for a short time
- **lobby:** entrance
- **overalls:** clothes you wear over your clothes to protect them while you are working
- **unloaded:** took goods off a vehicle

'Well, I hope they move that van soon – we can't see what's going on.' said Peters.

The two men watched as the workers continued to unload the van. At a quarter to six, it was driven away and parked behind the hotel.

'Fifteen minutes to go,' said Peters. 'Oh, look! There's Wilson.'

Hunter saw Slim Wilson standing at the hotel entrance, looking out over the car park. He was dressed in a very smart• suit• and he was holding his briefcase. Suddenly, he went back inside and said something to the receptionist•. Then he went and sat down on a sofa.

'He's waiting for the contact to arrive,' said Peters. 'With our lovely money!'

'Yeah!' said Hunter. 'I've got a ticket to the States• in my pocket. I'm catching a plane from here at eleven o'clock and then a flight to New York from Heathrow• at four this afternoon. Bye-bye Britain! Hello new life of luxury!'

The two men laughed. They watched as a lot of cars and vans drove into the car park and filled up most of the available spaces. Men in dark suits got out and walked over to the hotel entrance.

'It's busy here this morning, isn't it?' remarked Peters. 'I don't like it. Too many people.'

'Don't worry, Peters!' said Hunter. 'It's just people arriving for the conference.'

Endgame

Nobody noticed• the police helicopter land at Manchester Airport at five thirty that morning. Nobody saw Detective Riley and George and Sarah Broad get out of it and get into a blue unmarked• police car that was waiting for them.

When the car pulled into the Grand Hotel car park and parked a little while later, Detective Riley explained what was happening. 'Can you see those men in white overalls? They're our people. They're pretending• to be conference organisers. Michael is in the white computer van over there on the right, and two of the criminals are with him. Wilson is waiting inside to meet the person who he's going to sell the nuclear secrets to.'

'I didn't know airport hotels were so busy at this time in the morning. Look at all those people!'

Riley smiled. 'They're police officers too, Mrs Broad. They're pretending to be doctors arriving for the conference. The plan is that all our men will fill the reception area so that Wilson and his client can't get away.'

'It's just like in one of those TV thrillers•,' said George, smiling.

- **noticed:** saw
- **pretending:** acting in a particular way because they want others to believe something is true when it is not

- **thrillers:** films full of adventure, excitement and suspense
- **unmarked:** with no writing to say it is a police car

At one minute to six a black limousine* stopped outside the hotel. A very elegantly dressed gentleman carrying a suitcase got out. He went into the reception area of the hotel and spoke to the receptionist, who pointed to the sofa where Slim Wilson was sitting. Wilson stood up, smiled, and the two men shook hands. Then they sat down and started talking. A minute or two later, Wilson took the Lion envelope out of his briefcase and handed it to the other man, who put his suitcase on the coffee table in front of them. They shook hands again. Then, twenty or thirty men, some in suits, some in overalls, suddenly seemed to appear from nowhere. They quickly surrounded Wilson and the other man, who had no chance of running away. They were handcuffed* and taken to a room at the back of the hotel.

At the same moment, more officers surrounded the limousine in the car park. Others pulled open the doors of the computer van where Hunter and Peters were sitting, speechless* with surprise. They led the two men away to one of the blue vans waiting in the car park.

Riley and the Broads immediately ran to the computer van. The detective found the key and opened the back door.

'Michael,' he shouted. 'Michael, where are you?'

'In here,' came a muffled* voice from inside the box.

Two policemen carefully lifted the box out, laid it on the ground and opened it. The morning sun shone directly into Michael's eyes and he blinked*. For a few minutes he couldn't see all the people standing around him, smiling.

'Michael!' Sarah was the first person to speak. 'Michael!' She hugged him tightly to her chest. Then George hugged both of them.

'Are you all right?' asked George.

'Yes, I'm fine,' said Michael, with a big smile on his face. 'But could someone untie my wings, please?'

'Oh, Michael! What happened to your lovely white feathers?' cried Sarah.

'Don't worry, Sarah! It's only dye. It'll soon wash out•,' replied Michael, putting his arm around her.

Michael and the Broads didn't go back to Shillan immediately. They stayed in a luxurious suite• in the best hotel in Manchester for a week because the police needed to question the boy. While they were there, they watched the episode of *Strange But True* about Michael on TV. The last two days of the week were filled with discussions about Michael's future. There were many decisions to make.

When the Broads, Michael and Dr Reed flew back to Shillan, two policemen went with them They were Michael's permanent bodyguards•, so Michael was able to spend the rest of the summer relaxing and enjoying himself. Then the end of August arrived and  it was time to move again.

Glossary

- **bodyguards:** people who protect somebody
- **suite:** set of rooms
- **wash out:** go away (after washing)

Epilogue

In early September the Broads and Michael moved to a village in the north of England and Michael joined the third year at the local secondary school. People accepted him without asking too many questions and he soon made lots of friends. Then, when he was eighteen, things changed. George died and Michael went to university to study Biology. He got a good degree• and went on to do• an MSc•. His thesis• was on the rare flowers of Shillan.

Then he returned to the village and lived with Sarah. When she died he got a job teaching Biology at his secondary school. His students always enjoyed his lessons on flight the most because he took them out onto the sports fields for real live demonstrations.

He flew for his own pleasure about once a week, but always when nobody was around to watch him. Dr Reed kept in touch and visited him once every three months to record details of any changes. Now we must leave the man who could fly where we found him – crossing the park on his way home to have his supper.

Glossary

- **degree:** qualification you get from a university
- **MSc:** Masters in Science
- **thesis:** long essay for a Masters
- **went on to do:** did something after something else

After Reading
Personal Response

1 What did you think of this story? Write a paragraph describing your reaction to it.

2 Write a 150-word summary of the story.

3 Which character did you like most, and which least? Why?

4 Which part of the story did you like best? Explain why.

5 Is there anything in the story that you would have liked to change? Can you think of any way to improve the story?

6 Does the story remind you of any other books you have read or films or TV series you've watched? If so, which ones, and why?

After Reading
Comprehension

1 **Explain who these people are, what they do and how they are connected to Michael. Write one sentence about each of them.**

a) George and Sarah Broad

They are the couple who find Michael and adopt him as their son.

b) Jeff Hunter

c) Richard Reed

d) Paul Salter

e) Slim Wilson

f) Detective Riley

2 **Explain why the doctors keep Michael at the hospital. Does Michael like being there?**

▷◁ 3 Do you think it was right or wrong for Michael to escape from the hospital? Discuss your reasons with a partner.

4 What happens after Michael escapes from the hospital? Describe the situation he finds at home.

▷◁ 5 Describe Michael's life on Shillan before he is kidnapped. Would you like to live like that? What are the advantages and disadvantages? Share in groups.

6 How did Wilson and his gang discover where Michael lived? Why was it important that Hunter remembered Michael's exact words to him?

7 What did Wilson want Michael to get for him? What is Wilson going to do with it when he gets it?

8 Who is inside the high-security building when Michael opens the door? What are they holding? Why?
▷◁ Use the same method to give a partner instructions.

9 Where does Wilson go after he gets the envelope? Who does he meet and why?

10 How are the police able to follow Wilson's gang and Michael?

11 How do the police manage to capture the criminals? Describe what happens at the hotel and how the police trick the criminals.

12 Do you think that Michael is happy at the end of the book?

After Reading

Characters

1 **Answer these questions about the names of people in the story:**

    a) Why does Sarah call the baby she finds Michael?
    b) What is 'Slim' Wilson's real name?
    c) What is the newsagent's name?
    d) Who is Mary?
    e) What do you know about Mr Smith?
    f) Who is the 'big man' who does exercises with Michael?
    g) Who are Sally Roberts and Paul Brown?

2 **Which of the people in Exercise 1 above are important in the story, and why? Which ones are not important to the story?**

3 **In different parts of the story, Michael is happy and unhappy. Give examples from the story and explain why he feels the way he does.**

4 **Who says the following things? When do they say them and who do they say them to?**

> **a)** Why do I have to be here? I'm sick of living in a hospital.

> **b)** What you did was very wrong. We told you Michael couldn't go home.

> **c)** I've had a phone call from my boss in London. The BBC have asked if they can make a film about Michael.

> **d)** Hey, Mickey! What are you doing?

> **e)** It's busy here this morning, isn't it? I don't like it. Too many people.

> **f)** Oh, Michael! What happened to your lovely white feathers?

5 Choose one of these characters and write a description of them.

a) Dr Richard Reed   c) Jeff Hunter
b) Slim Wilson   d) Detective Riley

6 What is Michael like at the beginning and end of the story (when he is an adult)? What is his life like? Do you think he's happy? Why/why not?

After Reading
Plot and theme

1 **Look at these four pictures and write the order in which they happen.**

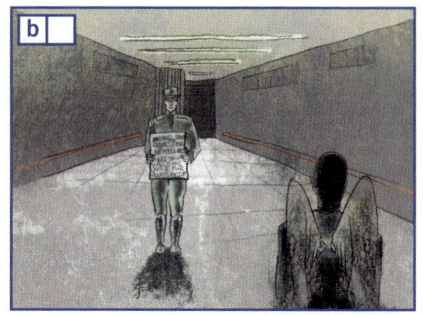

2 **Now write a sentence about what is happening in each of them.**

3 **Who tells this story?**

a) Michael

b) An external narrator

c) Another character from the story.

Find examples from the story to explain your choice.

4 How are the first and last chapters different from the others? What is the effect of this? Is it a good idea? Why/why not?

5 What are the main events in the story? Write them below.

The Broads find Michael on their doorstep

....

....

....

....

....

....

....

The police find Michael at the Grand Hotel, Manchester

6 What is the most exciting part of the story? Why?

7 Do you think the story has a happy ending? If so, what makes it happy? If not, why not?

8 What do you think about the way Michael is treated by the doctors and the police?

9 What are the main themes of the story? Choose two below and in groups find examples. Think of examples of them in real life.

- Difference
- Crime doesn't pay
- Media
- Integration
- Institutions
- Trust
- Town life versus life in isolation

After Reading

Language

1 Unscramble these words connected to flying. Write if the words are the nouns or verbs.

a) ria ....

d) giwn ....

b) ratfehe ....

e) tgifhl ....

c) revoh ....

f) lyf ....

2 Put the verbs in the box into the simple past then write them in the correct spaces.

fly	hover	land	open	rise

a) Michael .... in circles above the park.

b) Michael moved his wings and slowly .... into the air.

c) Michael .... his lovely white wings.

d) Michael .... in the same place without moving.

e) Michael was getting dizzy, so he .... in the park.

3 Write the words in the correct order to make sentences.

a) on / family / Shillan / to / the / live / moved
The family moved to live on Shillan..............................

b) every / Dr Reed / Michael / day / exercises / filmed / doing
....

c) Biology / was / Michael / very / in / interested
....

d) discovered / Wilson's / police / was / gang / where / the
....

e) take / Michael / envelope / Wilson / to / an / wanted
....

f) clothes / Michael / made / for / special / Sarah
....

4 Write one of the adjectives in the box into the correct sentence.

happy   frightened   worried   beautiful   rare

a) Michael, Sarah and George were very .... when they moved to Shillan.

b) Michael grew .... white feathers on his wings.

c) Michael studied the .... flowers of Shillan for his Biology project.

d) Sarah was very .... when Michael didn't come home for tea.

e) Michael was .... when Wilson told him what he had to do.

5 Complete the sentences with adverbs. Use the adjectives in brackets.

1 *Slowly*, Michael found that he could move his wings. (slow)

2 Michael moved his wings .... backwards and forwards. (gentle)

3 The three men walked .... down Castle Hill towards Michael. (silent)

4 The Broads .... told the police about finding the baby. (immediate)

5 Michael was surprised when he .... rose in the air for the first time. (sudden)

6 Jeff was .... trying to be friendly to Michael. (obvious)

6 Make questions and answers in the past simple.

a) what / Sarah / do / on Shillan / ?

b) when / Michael / grow / wings / ?

c) how / Michael / escape / from hospital / ?

d) what / want / Wilson / steal / Michael / ?

e) who / discover / where / Michael / live / ?

7 Now ask and answer the questions in Exercise 6 with a partner.

After Reading

1 Read this description of Michael Broad's life as an adult, and choose the most suitable word for each space.

At university, Michael studied Biology, and after Sarah died, he got a job teaching the **(a)** .... at his old secondary school. He was very **(b)** .... in flowers, and wrote many articles on the wild plants of the north of England. He often went away at the weekend to places in the hills and valleys to **(c)** .... wild flowers and photograph them. Sometimes, to save time, he **(d)** .... around. This was a good way of **(e)** .... time – he was able to fly to the top of a hill in about five minutes, when a walk took him over an hour. Of course, he **(f)** .... seeing all the flowers on the way up when he flew, so he usually walked. At school Michael was a very **(g)** .... teacher, and the students loved it when he taught them about flight. Then he took the students outside and **(h)** .... them the things he told them about in class.

a)	**1** object	**2** material	**3** subject
b)	**1** interesting	**2** interest	**3** interested
c)	**1** study	**2** watch	**3** look
d)	**1** flow	**2** flew	**3** flied
e)	**1** save	**2** to save	**3** saving
f)	**1** hadn't	**2** didn't	**3** wasn't
g)	**1** popular	**2** like	**3** friend
h)	**1** watched	**2** saw	**3** showed

2 Imagine you are Michael. You are in the hotel in Manchester. The police want you to write down what happened to you when you were with Slim Wilson's gang. Write about everything from when they shot you on Shillan until when the police set you free at the Grand Hotel in Manchester. Use your own words.

3 Read the sentences. Then tick (✔).

		T	F
a)	George and Sarah Broad are Michael's natural parents.	☐	☐
b)	When Michael is 12 years old, he grows wings.	☐	☐
c)	Michael lives in a hospital for a long time.	☐	☐
d)	The newspaper and TV reporters help Michael escape from hospital.	☐	☐
e)	Michael, Sarah and George go and live on a farm in the north of England.	☐	☐
f)	The cameraman from the BBC is also a criminal.	☐	☐
g)	The gang use Michael because he can fly into a building they can't enter.	☐	☐
h)	The police catch the gang at the Nuclear Complex near Leeds.	☐	☐

4 Look at the picture (page 75) and ask a partner questions about what you can see in it.

After Reading
Project

Flight

In groups make a poster, or a booklet or a presentation on ONE of the following.

a) How birds fly

Find out about:

- the physical features that birds have (e.g. wings, feathers, muscles, bones)
- how they move their wings when they fly
- different ways of flying
- how fast and how far birds can fly

b) The history of human flight

Find out about:

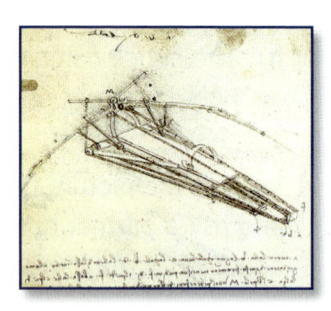

- early attempts, and stories (e.g. Icarus)
- Leonardo Da Vinci's drawings and experiments
- the first balloons (e.g. the Montgolfier brothers)
- the first powered flight (e.g. the Wright brothers)
- the development of jet engines
- supersonic flight (e.g. Concorde)